GET  MAKOTO+

EVERY MONTH AUTOMATICALLY
(and at a discount)

https://www.MakotoPlus.com

You'll get:

Download the Latest Makoto Issue | Weekly Lessons | Reusable TheJapanShop.com Coupon | Monthly Freebies

THEJAPANSHOP.COM
VOLUME 5 | ISSUE 52 | June 2022

誠 MAKOTO

e-zine for learners of Japanese

ご購入
ありがとう
ございます。

Thank you so much for your purchase!

夏休み is here! It seems it was just last week when I typed those same words 12 issues ago.

While Groucho Marx 's pun, "Time flies like an arrow; fruit flies like an apple" isn't easily translated into Japanese, Japanese does have:

光陰矢のごとし

Time flies like an arrow.

光陰 is a poetic term for "time," 矢 means "arrow," and ごとし means "like" or "as if," or "the same as." The older I get, the faster that 矢 flies!

If you are a student (or teacher) and find yourself with extra time this summer, make a few goals for improving your Japanese. Maybe you don't have time off from work like you did during your school days, but that doesn't mean you also can't come up with some special plan for the summer. Do something that will move you closer to your goal of fluency. みなさん、がんばりましょう！

Thank you!
Clay & Yumi

P.S. The cover says, 一緒に読もう *issho ni yomou*, which means, "Let's read together!" The words on the cover are: 調律 (tuning); 音楽 (music); 山葉寅楠 (Yamaha Torakusu); 音符 (musical notes); オルガン (organ)

In this Issue:

- **Laughs, Jokes, Riddles, and Puns**
- **Vocabulary: 血も涙もない**
- **Prefecture Spotlight: Nagano**
- **Etymology: デカ**
- **Anime Phrase of the Day**
- **Haiku : 夏目漱石**
- **Kanji Spotlight: 人**
- **Grammar Time! だけ**
- **Japanese Readers: Japanese Pancakes (beginner) + Yamaha (Intermediate)**

LAUGHS, JOKES, RIDDLES, AND PUNS

Q.日本人は物事を白黒つけるのが下手だと思いますか？

・思う２１ ％

・思わない ７ ％

・どちらともいえない ７２ ％

Scan for Recording

Question: Do you think Japanese people are not good at making definite, black-or-white decisions?

Answers:

- I think so: 21%

- I don't think so: 7%

- I can't say either: 72%

Vocabulary:

ジョーク *jo-ku*—a joke

日本人 *nihonjin*—Japanese person/people

は *wa*—(indicates the sentence topic)

物事 *monogoto*—things; everything

を *o*—(indicates the direct object of action)

白黒つける *shiro kuro tsukeru*—to make definite decisions; to determine whether something is right or wrong; to make something clear; to settle a matter [**白黒** (black and white; right

Vocabulary Continued

and wrong) + **つける** (determine; get into; put on; apply)]

の *no*—(nominalizer) [turns the part preceding it into a noun phrase]

が *ga*—(indicates the object of emotion)

下手 *heta*—bad; poor; not good

だと思います *da to omoimasu*—to think...; I think...; you think... [how to form: Noun + **だ** ＋ **と 思います**]

か *ka*—(question marker)

思う 21% *omou nijuu ichi pa-sento*—(I) think so: 21% [**思う** (to think; to consider)]

思わない 7% *omowanai nana pa-sento*—(I) don't think so: 7% [**思わない** is the plain negative form of **思う** (to think; to consider)]

どちらともいえない 72% *dochira to mo ienai nanajuu ni pa-sento*—(I) can't say either: 72% [**ど ちらともいえない** ((I am) not sure, (I) can't say which)]

VOCABULARY

Learn Useful Words, Phrases, and Sayings

Scan for Recording

^ち血も^{なみだ}涙もない

chi mo namida mo nai

cold-blooded; hardhearted; unfeeling; inhuman

ⓘ Used when someone is cold, unfeeling, or insusceptible to pity.

> Literally, "without blood or tears." A similar expression is 人でなし *hito de nashi* - inhuman; a brute; a monster.

EXAMPLE SENTENCE:

Example Sentence

こんなやさしい人を殺すなんて、

犯人は血も涙もないやつだ。

konna yasashii hito o korosu nante, hannin wa chi mo namida mo nai yatsu da.

To have killed such a nice person, the murderer is inhuman.

VOCABULARY:

こんな~ *konna~* —such as~

やさしい *yasashii*—kind

人 *hito*—person

殺す *korosu*—to kill

Vocabulary Continued

なんて *nante*—[colloquial variation of とは (quotation marker + topic marker) which quotes something that the speaker thinks is outrageous in either a good or bad sense before stating his or her own opinion about it. なんて is like an exclamation mark. It almost acts as the "that" in "How horrible **that** the man killed......." (not quite exact translation but hopefully you get the idea).]

犯人 *hannin*—criminal; the offender

血 *chi*—blood

も *mo*—even (blood/tears)

涙 *namida*—tears

血も涙もない *chi mo namida mo nai*—inhuman; cold-blooded [~もない means "there is even no ~"]

やつ *yatsu*—guy (usually with a negative sense)

だ *da*—plain form of です (be; is; means a word that links subjects and predicates)

ながの

Nagano 長野

Japanese: 長野県 *nagano ken*

Capital: 長野 Nagano

Population: 2,052,493 (June 1, 2019)

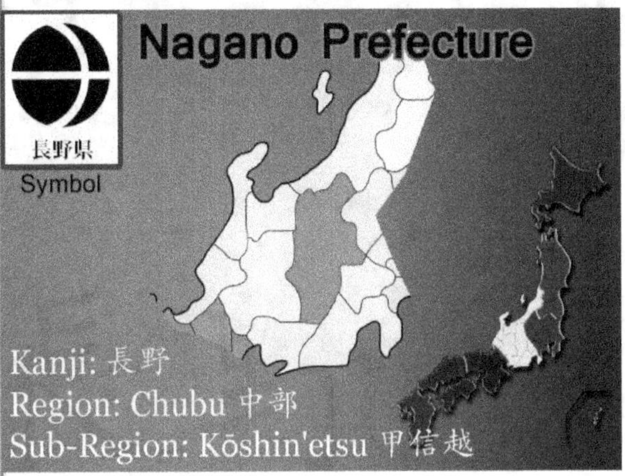

DID YOU KNOW?

Nagano was host to the 1998 Winter Olympics and borders more prefectures than any other prefecture in Japan.

PLACES TO SEE:

- **Matsumoto Castle**—one of Japan's most beautiful and original castles. It was originally built from 1592 to 1614. It has the oldest five-storied wooden *donjon* (castle keep) in the country.

- **Jigokudani Wild Monkey Park**—see wild monkeys bathe in an *onsen*.

- **Tsumago-juku**—a town preserved to look much as it did during the feudal Edo Period.

- **Kamikochi**—a resort in the Northern Japan Alps sporting beautiful mountain scenery. It is closed in the winter.

- **Kiso Valley**—an area that was once an important trade route. The buildings have been preserved to look and feel as they did in the Edo period.

- **Karuizawa**—an often pricy mountain resort near the active volcano Mt. Asama.

FAMOUS FOR:

- The **world-class ski resorts** at Hakuba and Shiga Kogen.

- The many mountains make it a popular place for **mountain resorts and hot springs.**

- **Japanese Alps**—nine of the twelve **highest mountains** in Japan are in Nagono.

- Nagano has one of the world's **highest geysers in Suwa** (about 40-50 meters or 131 to 164 feet).

- **Nagano apples**—second largest producer of apples in Japan. Aomori prefecture is number one.

- **Shinano soba**—Nagano's buckwheat noodles.

長野

「デカ」

"deka"

Scan for Recording

犯罪を捜査する刑事さんのことを俗語で「デカ」と言います。明治時代、警察官で制服を着ていない刑事は和服を着ていました。和服の袖は四角い形をしているので、「角袖」と言いました。角袖の刑事、最後の「で」と最初の「か」をとって、「デカ」と呼んでいました。こういう言い方をしていたのは犯罪者たちで、一般の人は使っていなかったのですが、時代とともにだんだんと広がって今では誰でも知っている言葉になりました。普段の会話ではあまり使いませんが、小説やドラマの中ではよく出てきますので、覚えておきましょう。

8

Continued

A slang term for a detective investigating a crime is called "deka". During the Meiji era (1868-1912), police detectives who did not wear uniforms wore kimono. The sleeves of kimono were square in shape, so they were called "kakusode (square sleeves)". The detective in *kakusode*, taking the last "de" and the first "ka", was called "deka". This way of speaking was used by criminals and not by the general public, but it gradually spread with the times and has now become a word that everyone knows. It is not used much in everyday conversation, but it often appears in novels and dramas, so let's remember it.

Vocabulary

語源 etymology; origin of a word

「デカ」 "deka" [「」 (quotation marks) + デカ (*deka*)]

犯罪を捜査する (a detective who) investigates a crime [犯罪 (crime; offense) + を (indicates the direct object of action) + 捜査する (investigate; conduct search)]

刑事さんのこと all the things about the detective [刑事さん ((police) detective; 刑事 (detective) + さん (politeness marker; is used after a noun or sometimes な-adjective)) + のこと (all the things about; it has a "focusing" feature and lets you know that the subject has a certain quality; how to form: Noun + のこと)]

俗語で in slang term [俗語 (slang term; colloquial language; slang) + で (in; by)]

「デカ」と言います is called "deka" [「デカ」 ("deka") + と言います (called; と (quotation marker) + 言います (polite/ます form of 言う (to say; to utter)))]

明治時代 Meiji period (1868-1912) [明治 (Meiji) + 時代 (period; epoch; era; age)]

警察官 police officer; policeman; policewoman

で (て-form of です (be; is) which is used to connect to the next phrase)

制服を着ていない刑事 detectives who do not wear uniforms [制服 (uniform) + を (indicates the direct object of action) + 着ていない (do not wear; plain negative form of 着ている (wear; wearing; ている form of 着る (to wear; to put on) which is used to describe the actual appearance of the subject)) + 刑事 ((police) detective)]

和服を着ていました wore a *kimono* [和服 (*kimono*; Japanese clothes) + を (indicates the direct object of action) + 着ていました (wore; polite past form of 着ている (wear; wearing; ている form of 着る (to wear; to put on); how to form: Verb て form + いる))]

Vocabulary Continued

和服の袖は the sleeves of *kimono* [和服 (*kimono*; Japanese clothes) + の (of; modifier) + 袖 (sleeve) + は (indicates the sentence topic)]

四角い形をしている square-shaped; have square appearance [四角い (square; rectangular) + 形 (form; shape; figure) + を (indicates the direct object of action) + している (ている form of する (to do; to be) which is used to describe the appearance of the subject)]

ので because of …; the reason is …; so

「角袖」と言いました was/were called "kakusode" [「角袖」("kakusode"; square sleeves) + と言いました (was/were called)]

角袖の刑事 detective in *kakusode* [角袖 (square sleeves; 角 (square; cube; angle) + 袖 (sleeve)) + の (in; modifier) + 刑事 ((police) detective)]

最後の「で」the last "de" [最後 (last; end) + の (of; modifier) + 「で」("de")]

と and

最初の「か」をとって taking the first "ka" [最初 (beginning; first) + の (of; modifier) + 「か」("ka") + を (indicates the direct object of action) + とって (taking; て-form of とる (to take) which is used to connect to the next phrase)]

「デカ」と呼んでいました was called "deka" [「デカ」("deka") + と呼んでいました (was called; と (quotation marker) + 呼んでいました (polite past form of 呼んでいる (ている form of 呼ぶ (to call) which is used to describe a continuous action)))]

こういう言い方をしていた put it this way; said in this way [こういう (such; this sort of; like this) + 言い方 (way of saying (something); way of putting it; wording; expression) + を (indicates the direct object of action) + していた (plain past form of している (ている form of する (to do) which is used to describe a continuous action))]

の (nominalizer) [turns the preceding clause into a noun phrase]

犯罪者たちで criminals [犯罪者たち (criminals; 犯罪者 (criminal; culprit) + たち (pluralizing suffix)) + で (て-form of です (be; is) which is used to connect to the next phrase)]

一般の人 general public [一般 (general; universal; common) + の (of; modifier) + 人 (person; people)]

使っていなかったのです was not used [使っていなかった (was not used; plain negative past form of 使っている (ている-form of 使う (to use))) + のです (shows emphasis; how to form: Verb (casual) + のです)]

Vocabulary Continued

が but; however

時代とともに with the times; in time [時代 (the times; those days; period) + とともに (with; together with; at the same time as; as well as ~); how to form: Noun + とともに]

だんだんと gradually; increasingly; in small steps

広がって spread and [て-form of 広がる (to spread (out); to extend) which is used to connect to the next phase, creating the meaning of "and"]

今では now [今 (now; the present time) + では (adds emphasis)]

誰でも anyone; anybody; everyone; everybody

知っている言葉になりました became a word that everyone knows [知っている (know; knowing; ている form of 知る (to know; to be aware (of)) which is used to describe a continuous action) + 言葉 (word; term; phrase) + に (expresses the result of change) + なりました (became; polite past form of なる (to become; to turn))]

普段の会話 everyday conversation [普段 (usual; normal; everyday; ordinary) + の (of; modifier) + 会話 (conversation; talk; chat)]

では in

あまり使いませんが (it) is not used much (in everyday conversation), but [あまり ((not) much) + 使いません (not use; polite negative form of 使う (to use)) + が (but; however)]

小説 novel; (short) story

や such things as ...; and ... and

ドラマの中では in dramas [ドラマ (drama) + の (of; modifier) + 中 (in; inside) + では (adds emphasis)]

よく出てきます (it) often appears [よく (frequently; often) + 出てきます (to come out; to appear)]

ので so; because of ...; the reason is ...

覚えておきましょう let's remember (it) [from 覚える (to remember; to bear in mind); ~ておきましょう is the polite volitional form of ~ておく (to do something in advance; how to form: Verb て-form + おく); volitional form of a verb is used when making a suggestion to one or more people including oneself ("let's" / "shall we")]

ANIME / MANGA PHRASE
Surprise your Japanese friends with these phrases

Scan for Recording

Please see the sound files for the pronunciation

「四月は君の嘘」

宮園かをりのセリフ

「君は君だよ。『君らしく』なんて曖昧なものじゃない。何やったって変わったってカンケーない。君はどうせ君だよ。」

「*shigatsu wa kimi no uso*」

miyazono kaori no serifu

kimi wa kimi da yo. 「*kimirashiku*」 *nante aimaina mono ja nai. nani yatta tte kawatta tte kanke– nai. kimi wa douse kimi da yo.*

"Your Lie in April"
Line from Miyazono Kaori
You're you. "To be like you" is not an ambiguous thing. No matter what you do, no matter how you change, it doesn't mean a thing. You're just you, after all.

ANIME / MANGA PHRASE

Surprise your Japanese friends with these phrases

Continued

VOCABULARY

「」 —(quotation marks; " ")

四月 *shigatsu*—April; fourth month in the lunar calendar [四 (four; 4) + 月 (month; moon)]

は *wa*—(indicates the sentence topic)

君の嘘 *kimi no uso*—your lie [君 (you; familiar language, sometimes considered male language; referring to someone of equal or lower status) + の (indicates possessive) + 嘘 (lie; fib; falsehood; untruth)]

宮園かをりのセリフ *miyazono kaori no serifu*—line from Miyazono Kaori [宮園かをり (Miyazono Kaori) + の (of; from; modifier) + セリフ (one's lines; speech; words)]

君は君だよ *kimi wa kimi da yo*—you are you [君 (you) + は (indicates the sentence topic) + 君 (you) + だよ (sentence ender showing assertion or confidence; is used in spoken Japanese and informal situations)]

『君らしく』なんて 『*kimirashiku*』 *nante*—"to be like you" [『』 (quotation marks) + 君らしく (to be like you; 君 (you) + らしく (continuative form of らしい (seem like; look like; it appears that; how to form: Noun + らしい))) + なんて (emphasizes the preceding phrase)]

曖昧な *aimaina*—ambiguous; vague; unclear

もの *mono*—thing; object; article; stuff; substance [indicates tangible things]

じゃない *ja nai*—is not; are not

13

ANIME / MANGA PHRASE

Surprise your Japanese friends with these phrases

Vocabulary Continued

何やったって *nani yatta tte*—no matter what (you) do [何 (what) + やったって (from やる (to do; to perform); ~たって means "no matter how; even if; even though"; how to form: Verb (casual, past) + って)]

変わったって *kawatta tte*—no matter how you change [from 変わる (to change); ~たって means "no matter how; even if; even though"]

カンケーない *kanke– nai*—to have nothing to do; no relation; unconnected; irrespective [カンケー (relation; very casual form of かんけい (relation; relationship; connection)) + ない (no; not)]

君は *kimi wa*—you [君 (you) + は (indicates the sentence topic)]

どうせ *douse*—after all; in any case; no matter what; at any rate

君だよ *kimi da yo*—you [君 (you) + だよ (sentence ender showing assertion or confidence)]

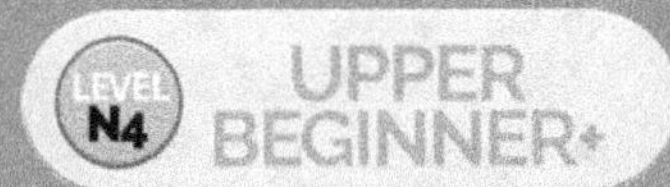

Natsume Souseki 夏目漱石（なつめそうせき）

かたまるや　散（ち）るや蛍（ほたる）の

川（かわ）の上（うえ）

Haiku Audio

katamaru ya / chiru ya hotaru no / kawa no ue
Clumping together and | Scattering | Fireflies on the river

Explanation:

Explanation

季語（きご）: 蛍（ほたる）

川（かわ）の上（うえ）で蛍（ほたる）がかたまったり、散（ち）ったりしています。

Season term: Fireflies

Fireflies are gathering together and scattering on the river.

HAIKU
Condensed Japanese Language and Culture

Continued

Vocabulary

かたまる to gather (together); to assemble; to clump

や and

散る to scatter; to be dispersed

蛍 firefly; glowworm; lightning bug

の (modifier)

川の上 on the river [川 (river; stream) + の (is used to tell the location; modifier) + 上 (above; up; top; on high)]

季語 seasonal word (in haiku)

川の上で on the river [川の上 (on the river) + で (indicates the location of action)]

が (emphasizes the preceding word 蛍 (firefly))

かたまったり、散ったりしています (fireflies) are clumping and scattering [from かたまる (to gather (together); to clump) and 散る (to scatter); 「たり～たりしています」 is the しています form (progressive form) of たり～たりする (means "and/or" which is used to list representative activities in which there may be additional activities that are not mentioned); how to form: Verb (た form) + り + Verb (た form) + り + しています]

夏目漱石 Natsume Souseki (February 1867 – December 1916) [He was a Japanese novelist, scholar of British literature and writer of haiku, *kanshi* (Chinese poetry), and fairy tales.]

KANJI SPOTLIGHT

Learning kanji one character at a time.

JLPT N5 Kanji

On: じん；にん

Kun: ひと

Meaning: person; people

Hint: This is a **person** with no head or arms trying to do a split.

Audio of Readings

Stroke Order:

人 ノ 人

Examples:

<ruby>日本人<rt>にほんじん</rt></ruby> a Japanese person [simply add a *"jin"* after many countries]

<ruby>大人<rt>おとな</rt></ruby> adult; a grown-up [this is an irregular reading]

<ruby>外国人<rt>がいこくじん</rt></ruby> foreigner

<ruby>美人<rt>びじん</rt></ruby> a beautiful woman

<ruby>宇宙人<rt>うちゅうじん</rt></ruby> a space alien

Audio of Example

あなたは<ruby>美人<rt>びじん</rt></ruby>です。

anata wa bijin desu.

You are a beautiful woman.

VOCABULARY:

あなた *anata*—you

は *wa*—(indicates the sentence topic)

美人 *bijin*—beautiful woman

です *desu*—be; is

だけ

Only; just

ABOUT:

When you want to limit how many or how much from a group, you can use だけ. *Only; just; merely; nothing but...*

HOW TO USE:

■ Place after the object or idea you wish to limit.

EXAMPLES:

試験に落ちたのは、私**だけ**だった。

Of those who failed the test, it was <u>only</u> me.

[私だけ could be, "I, alone" or "just me" or "I was the only one..."]

もう一回**だけ**、あの山に登りたい。

I want to climb that mountain <u>**just one**</u> more time.

[Only one time; just once]

Example 1

Example 2

18

Continued

It can also be used for downplaying something's significance. *It's merely... It is only a...*

あの料理^{りょうり}は、いいにおいがする**だけ**。おいしくないです。

That food smells good. **That's all**. It doesn't taste good.

[It *only* smells good.]

Example 3

VOCABULARY:

試験 *shiken*—examination; exam; test

に *ni*—(expresses the object of the verb)

落ちた *ochita*—failed [plain past form of 落ちる (to fail (e.g. exam or class); to fall down)]

の *no*—(a nominalizer that acts like a noun)

は *wa*—(indicates the sentence topic)

私 *watashi*—I; me

だけ *dake*—only; just; merely; simply; no more than; nothing but; alone; as much as; to the extent of; enough to

だった *datta*—was; were [plain past form of です (be; is)]

もう一回 *mou ikkai*—one more time; once more; once again [もう (more; again; another) + 一回 (one

Vocabulary Continued

time; once; one round)]

あの *ano*—that; those; the

山 *yama*—mountain; hill

に *ni*—to; into; at; in (expresses the direction and destination)

登りたい *noboritai*—want to climb [from 登る (to climb; to go up); ~たい means "want to do something";
how to form: Verb ます (stem form) + たい]

あの料理 *ano ryouri*—that food [あの (that; the; those) + 料理 (food; dish; cooking; meal)]

いいにおいがする *ii nioi ga suru*—give off a nice smell; (that food) smells good [いい (good; nice; pleas-
ant) + におい (scent; smell) + がする (to smell; hear; taste; how to form: Noun + がする)]

おいしくない *oishikunai*—(it) doesn't taste good [from おいしい (good(-tasting); delicious; tasty); ~くない
functions like "not" in English; how to form: drop the ~い ending from an い-adjective and replace it with
く then add ない]

です *desu*—be; is

よんでみよう！LET'S READ!

Learn through reading for (very) beginners of Japanese

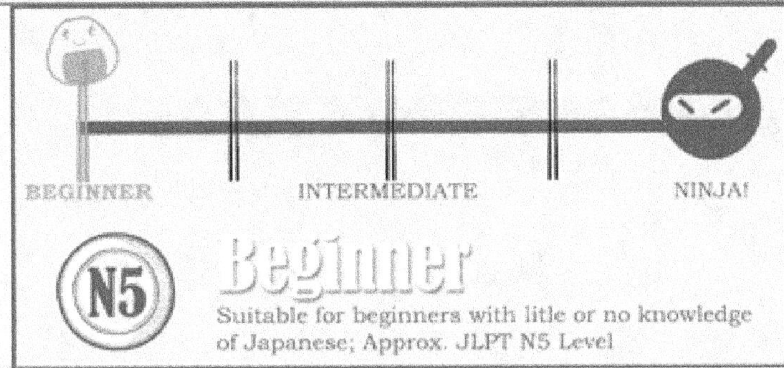

Have you only recently learned hiragana but need practice? Or perhaps, your hiragana is no problem, but you want to build your reading comprehension?

This segment is here to the rescue!

Read real Japanese—beginner level but not boring Japanese! Enjoy reading flash fiction, super short essays, and funny stories of common mistakes made by foreigners in Japan.

Best of all, the only requirement is that you can read hiragana. Vocabulary and grammar will be defined and explained.

The format is a little different from our other more advanced readers. The idea is for the reader to read the entire story three times. Each page will have a sentence or two in hiragana (with spaces between words for you to see "words" instead of syllables) at the top and that same content in full Japanese (with furigana) at the bottom. The middle will have the glossary and grammatical explanations. Lastly, the story will be presented in Japanese without furigana. See if you can read it after going through the explanations.

If you have just learned hiragana, you may want to listen to the sound file while reading the hiragana section to practice correct pronunciation. If you have studied Japanese a bit longer, you may want to start with the bottom version and take note of the glossary for understanding.

Makoto+ members can access this in a more interactive format. To learn more:

http://MakotoPlus.com

And now...

Let's learn about...

JAPANESE PANCAKES

Normal Speed

Slow Speed

Normal Speed

Slow Speed

The top and bottom Japanese texts are identical in meaning. The top version is only in hiragana and includes spaces between words. The bottom version has no spaces and uses kanji with furigana. Unless you are just practicing hiragana recognition, try to work through both versions. Scan the QR codes for the sound files.

日本のパンケーキ

JAPANESE PANCAKES

にほん　の　ぱんけーき　は、あめりか　の　ぱんけーき　と　ちょっと　ちがいます。とても　ふわふわ　で　やわらかい　です。

GLOSSARY AND NOTES

日本のパンケーキ *nihon no panke-ki*—Japanese pancake [日本の　(Japanese; 日本 (Japan) + の (of; 's; modifier)) + パンケーキ (pancake)]

は　*wa*—(indicates the sentence topic)

アメリカのパンケーキ *amerika no panke-ki*—American pancake [アメリカの　(American; アメリカ (United States of America; United States; US; USA) + の　('s; of; modifier)) + パンケーキ (pancake)]

と　*to*—with; and; as [connecting particle]

ちょっと　*chotto*—somewhat; a bit; a little; slightly

違います　*chigaimasu*—to differ (from); to be different; to be distinct

とても　*totemo*—very; awfully; exceedingly

ふわふわでやわらかい　*fuwafuwa de yawarakai*—fluffy and soft [ふわふわ　(soft; fluffy; spongy) + で　(て-form of です　(be; is) which is used to connect to the next phrase, creating the meaning of "and") + やわらかい　(soft; tender)]

です　*desu*—be; is

日本のパンケーキは、アメリカのパンケーキとちょっと違います。とてもふわふわでやわらかいです。

どうして　でしょう　か？　じつ　は、つくりかた　が　ちがいます。
まず、たまご　の　しろみ　を　あわだてて　めれんげ　を　つくりま
す。これ　に　こむぎこ　と　たまご　を　いれて　まぜます。

GLOSSARY AND NOTES

どうして　*doushite*—why; for what reason

でしょうか　*deshou ka*—(polite question marker)

実は　*jitsu wa*—actually; as a matter of fact; in reality; fact is [実 (truth; reality) + は (adds emphasis)]

作り方が違います　*tsukurikata ga chigaimasu*—the way to make (it) is different [作り方 (how to make) + が (emphasizes the preceding word; identifies what performs the action) + 違います (to differ (from); to be different; to be distinct)]

まず　*mazu*—first (of all); firstly; to begin with

たまごの白身　*tamago no shiromi*—whites of eggs; egg whites [たまご (eggs; egg; spawn; roe) + の (of; modifier) + 白身 (white meat; egg white)]

を　*o*—(indicates the direct object of action)

泡立てて　*awadatete*—whip [て-form of 泡立てる (to beat (e.g. eggs); to whip (e.g. cream); to whisk) which is used to connect to the next phrase]

メレンゲを作ります　*merenge o tsukurimasu*—make meringue [メレンゲ (meringue) + を (indicates the direct object of action) + 作ります (ます/polite form of 作る (to make; to produce))]

これに　*kore ni*—in this; on this; hereto; to this [これ (this) + に (in; to; on)]

小麦粉とたまご　*komugiko to tamago*—flour and eggs [小麦粉 (flour; wheat flour) + と (and) + たまご (egg)]

入れて混ぜます　*irete mazemasu*—put and stir up [入れて (put and; て-form of 入れる (to put in; to let in) which is used to connect to the next verb 混ぜます) + 混ぜます (to mix; to stir; to blend)]

どうしてでしょうか？　実は、作り方が違います。まず、たま
ごの白身を泡立ててメレンゲを作ります。これに小麦粉とたま
ごを入れて混ぜます。

それ　から、そっと　ふらいぱん　に　いれて　やきます。にほん　の
ぱんけーき　は、あめりか　の　ぱんけーき　の　に　ばい　くらい
の　たかさ　まで　ふくらみます。あなた　も　ぜひ　つくって　みて
ください。

GLOSSARY AND NOTES

それから *sore kara*—and then; after that; then

そっと *sotto*—softly; gently; lightly

フライパンに入れて焼きます *furaipan ni irete yakimasu*—put in a frying pan and bake (it) [フライパン (frying pan) + に (in) + 入れて (put and; て-form of 入れる (to put in; to let in) which is used to connect to the next verb 焼きます) + 焼きます (to bake; to roast; to toast)]

アメリカのパンケーキの2倍くらいの高さ *amerika no panke-ki no ni bai kurai no takasa*—about twice the height of American pancakes [アメリカの (American) + パンケーキ (pancake) + の (of; modifier) + 2倍 (double; twice (as much); twofold) + くらい (about; around; approximately) + 高さ (height; altitude)]

まで *made*—to; up to

膨らみます *fukuramimasu*—to expand; to swell (out); to get big

あなた *anata*—you

も *mo*—too; also

ぜひ *zehi*—certainly; without fail; please; definitely

作ってみてください *tsukutte mite kudasai*—try making (it); please try to make (it) [from 作る (to make; to prepare (food)); ~てみてください is used to express a demand, suggestion to someone to do something for the first time; how to form: Verb て-form + みてください]

それから、そっとフライパンに入れて焼きます。日本のパンケーキは、アメリカのパンケーキの2倍くらいの高さまで膨らみます。あなたもぜひ作ってみてください。

日本のパンケーキ

JAPANESE PANCAKES

Now, let's read the story once more in natural Japanese.
Lastly, check the English translation to make sure you understand.

　日本のパンケーキは、アメリカのパンケーキとちょっと違います。とてもふわふわでやわらかいです。どうしてでしょうか？実は、作り方が違います。まず、たまごの白身を泡立ててメレンゲを作ります。これに小麦粉とたまごを入れて混ぜます。それから、そっとフライパンに入れて焼きます。日本のパンケーキは、アメリカのパンケーキの２倍くらいの高さまで膨らみます。あなたもぜひ作ってみてください。

ENGLISH: (try to save this for last)

　Japanese pancakes are somewhat different from American pancakes. They are very fluffy and soft. Why is that? Actually, the way to make it is different. First, whip the whites of eggs to make meringue. Add flour and eggs to this mixture and stir it up. Then gently put it in a frying pan and bake it. Japanese pancakes expand to about twice the height of American pancakes. You should try making them too.

KEY VOCABULARY

日本のパンケーキ *nihon no panke-ki*—Japanese pancake [日本の (Japanese; 日本 (Japan) + の (of; 's; modifier)) + パンケーキ (pancake)]

アメリカのパンケーキ *amerika no panke-ki*—American pancake

ふわふわでやわらかい *fuwafuwa de yawarakai*—fluffy and soft

違います *chigaimasu*—to differ (from)

たまごの白身 *tamago no shiromi*—whites of eggs; egg whites

メレンゲ *merenge*—meringue

小麦粉とたまご *komugiko to tamago*—flour and eggs

フライパン *furaipan*—frying pan

膨らみます *fukuramimasu*—to expand; to swell (out); to get big

JAPANESE READER

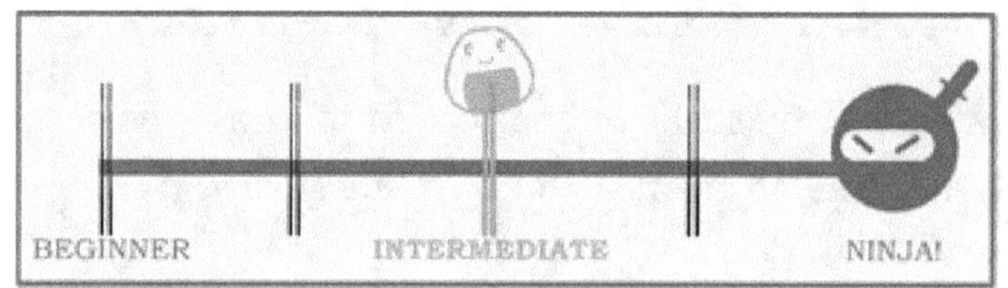

ヤマハ

Yamaha

Story Read Normal

Story Read Slow Speed

Yamaha Torakusu (1851-1916), founder of Yamaha Corporation.

Work through the story, sentence-by-sentence, referring to the vocabulary and grammar explanations below as needed.

ヤマハという会社を知っていますか？音楽を勉強した人、ピア

ノを習ったことのある人は、良く知っていると思います。ピア

ノの販売量が世界一の会社です。

ヤマハ Yamaha Corporation

という named; called [is used to define, describe, and generally just talk about the thing itself]

会社 company; corporation

を (indicates the direct object of action)

知っています know; knowing [ています-form of 知る (to know; to be familiar with) which is used to describe some continuous action or events; how to use: Verb て-form + います]

か (question marker)

音楽を勉強した人 a person who studied music [音楽 (music) + を (indicates the direct object of action) + 勉強した (studied; plain past form of 勉強する (study)) + 人 (person; people)]

ピアノを習った learned piano; took piano lessons [ピアノ (piano) + を (indicates ピアノ as the direct object of action) + 習った (learned; plain past form of 習う (to take lessons in; to learn; to study))]

こと (talks about an action or activity) [Using the past tense of the verb with 「こと」, you can talk about whether an action or activity has ever taken place.]

のある人は the person who (studied music or have taken piano lessons) [のある (adjectival clause which is used to describe the kind of 人 (person)) + 人 (person; people) + は (indicates the sentence topic)]

良く知っている know (it) well [良く (well; properly) + 知っている (know; ている-form of 知る (to know; to be familiar with) which is used to describe some continuous action or events)]

と思います to think…; I think…; you think…

ピアノの販売量が the sales volume of pianos [ピアノ (piano) + の (of; modifier) + 販売量 (sales volume) + が (emphasizes the preceding word; identifies what performs the action)]

世界一の会社 the company with the largest (sales volume of pianos) in the world [世界一 (number one in the world; world's largest; 世界 (the world) + 一 (one; best; first)) + の (of; 's; modifier) + 会社 (company; corporation)]

です be; is

ヤマハは、明治時代、山葉寅楠という人が始めました。きっか

けは、オルガンの修理でした。　１　８　８　７年、山葉寅楠

は、ある小学校からオルガンの修理を頼まれました。アメリカ

製のオルガンでした。

明治時代 Meiji period (1868-1912) [明治 (Meiji) + 時代 (period; epoch; era; age)]

山葉寅楠という人が a man named Yamaha Torakusu [山葉寅楠 (Yamaha Torakusu; founder of the Yamaha Corporation) + という (named) + 人 (man; person) + が (identifies who performs the action)]

始めました started [polite past form of 始める (to start; to begin; to originate)]

きっかけは chance; start; trigger; motivator [きっかけ (is the incident/action that leads to a consequence or the current state/situation) + は (adds emphasis; indicates the sentence topic)]

オルガンの修理 repair of organ (musical instrument) [オルガン (organ) + の (of; modifier) + 修理 (repair; mending; fixing)]

でした was/were [polite past tense marker; polite past form of です (be; is); how to form: Noun + でした]

１８８７年 year 1887 [年 (year)]

ある小学校 a certain elementary school [ある (a certain; some) + 小学校 (primary school; elementary school; grade school)]

から from; by

オルガンの修理を頼まれました (he) was asked to repair an organ [オルガン (organ) + の (of; modifier) + 修理 (repair; mending; fixing) + を (indicates the direct object of action) + 頼まれました (polite passive positive past form of 頼む (to request; to beg; to ask))]

アメリカ製のオルガンでした (it) was an American-made organ [アメリカ製 (American-made; アメリカ (United States of America; United States; US; USA) + 製 (-made; make)) + の (of; 's; modifier) + オルガン (organ) + でした (was; polite past tense marker)]

山葉は、時計の修理などを勉強していたので、このオルガンを

修理します。そのとき、オルガンの構造を見て、自分で作ってみ

ようと思いました。その頃、オルガンはすべて外国製でとても

高価でした。

時計の修理 repair of watch [時計 (clock; watch; time-

piece) + の (of; modifier) + 修理 (repair)]

など et cetera; etc.; and the like; and so forth

勉強していた had studied; was/were studying; has/have

been studying [plain past form of 勉強している

(studying; ている-form of 勉強する (to study) which is

used to describe a continuous action)]

ので since; because; the reason is …

このオルガンを修理します repair this organ [この

(this; that; these) + オルガン (organ) + を (indicates

the direct object of action) + 修理します (repair; fix)]

そのとき at that time; at that moment; then; on that

occasion [その (that; the) + とき (time; moment)]

オルガンの構造を見て see the structure of the organ

and [オルガン (organ) + の (of; modifier) + 構造

(structure; construction) + を (indicates the direct

object of action) + 見て (て-form of 見る (to see; to

look; to watch) which is used to connect to the next

phrase, creating the meaning of "and")]

自分で by oneself; by myself; in person

作ってみようと思いました thought to try building

(one himself) [作ってみよう (from 作る (to make; to

produce); ~てみよう is the volitional form of ~てみ

る (try to (do something)); volitional form is used

when the speaker initiates an act; how to form: Verb

て-form + みよう) + と思いました (thought; polite

past form of と思う (to think…; I think…; you

think…))]

その頃 at that time; in those days [その (that; the) +

頃 (time)]

すべて everything; all; the whole

外国製でとても高価でした was/were foreign-made

and very expensive [外国製 (foreign-made) + で

(and; て-form of です (be; is) which is used to con-

nect to the next phrase, creating the meaning of

"and") + とても (very; exceedingly) + 高価 (highly

priced; expensive; costly) + でした (was/were)]

このオルガンは当時４５円（今の約９０万）でした。で

も、山葉は、「自分なら3円で作ってみせる！」と言ったそうで

す。そして、言ったとおり、1年後に日本で初めての国産のオル

ガンを作りました。

このオルガンは this organ [この (this; that; these) + オ
ルガン (organ) + は (indicates the sentence topic)]

当時45円（今の約90万）でした cost 45 yen at that
time (about 900,000 today) [当時 (at that time; in
those days) + 45円 (45 yen; 円 (Japanese monetary
unit)) + 今の (as of now; of today; 今 (now; the present time) + の (of)) + 約90万 (about 900,000; 約
(approximately; about) + 90万 (900,000; 万 (ten thou-
sand))) + でした (polite past tense marker)]

でも but; however

「自分なら3円で作ってみせる！」と言った (Yamaha)
said, "I'll make it myself for 3 yen!" [「」 (quotation
marks; " ") + 自分 (myself; yourself; oneself; himself;
herself) + なら (emphasizes the preceding word 自分;
expresses one's ability or characteristic) + 3円 (3 yen;
円 (Japanese monetary unit)) + で (indicates a total or
an extent; is placed after a quantity, time, or amount
of money) + 作ってみせる (from 作る (to make; to
produce); ~てみせる means "I'll do my best; I'll definitely do"; how to form: Verb て-form + みせる) + と

(quotation marker) + 言った (said; plain past form of
言う (to say; to utter))]

そうです it is said that ~; (I) heard that ~; it appears
[how to form: Verb (casual form) + そうです]

そして and; and then; thus

言ったとおり as (I) said; (he) was right [from 言う (to
say; to utter); ~とおり means "as; in the same way as";
how to form: Verb (casual, past) + とおり]

1年後に a year later [1年 (a year; one year) + 後 (after;
later) + に (specifies the time)]

日本で in Japan [日本 (Japan) + で (at; in; indicates the
location of action)]

初めての国産のオルガン first domestically produced
organ [初めて (first; for the first time) + の (of; modifier) + 国産 (domestically produced; domestic; Japa-
nese-made) + オルガン (organ)]

作りました made; created; produced [polite past form
of 作る (to make; to produce; to build)]

ところが、学校で先生たちに弾いてもらうと、「あまりいい音が

しません。」と言われてしまいます。山葉は、東京の音楽取り

調べ所（今の東京芸術大学）まで自作のオルガンを運んで、

ところが however; on the contrary

学校で at school [学校 (school) + で (at; indicates the location of action)]

先生たちに弾いてもらう (he) had the teachers play (the organ) [先生たち (teachers; たち is a pluralizing suffix especially for people and animals) + に (shows who you're requesting to do the task) + 弾いてもらう ("play for me" or "have someone play"; from 弾く (to play (a stringed or keyboard instrument)); ~てもらう means "to get somebody to do something"; how to form: Verb て-form + もらう)]

と when; if

「あまりいい音がしません」 "(it) doesn't sound very good" [「」 (quotation marks; " ") + あまり ((not) very; (not) much) + いい (good; fine; nice) + 音 (sound) + (が)しません (polite negative form of 「(が)する」 (to smell; to hear; to taste))]

と言われてしまいます (they) said; told [と (quotation marker) + 言われてしまいます (from 言われる (plain passive positive form of 言う (to say; to utter)); ~てしまいます (refers to a regrettable event or negative meaning); how to form: Verb て-form + しまいます)]

東京の音楽取り調べ所 Music Investigation Office in Tokyo [東京 (Tokyo) + の (in; of; modifier) + 音楽取り調べ所 (Music Investigation Office)]

今の東京芸術大学 now Tokyo University of the Arts [今 (now; the present time) + の (modifier) + 東京芸術大学 (Tokyo University of the Arts; Tokyo National University of Fine Arts and Music)]

東京の音楽取り調べ所（今の東京芸術大学）まで to the Music Investigation Office in Tokyo (now Tokyo University of the Arts) [東京の音楽取り調べ所 (Music Investigation Office in Tokyo) + 今の東京芸術大学 (now Tokyo University of the Arts) + まで (to (a place); up to; as far as)]

自作のオルガンを運んで carry his self-made organ [自作 (one's own work; making by oneself) + の ('s; of; indicates possessive) + オルガン (organ) + を (indicates the direct object of action) + 運んで (て-form of 運ぶ (to carry; to transport; to move; to convey) which is used to connect to the next phrase)]

どうしていい音がでないのか、調べてもらいました。その当時^{とうじ}

は、自動車も電車も走っていませんから、オルガンを担いで

東京まで歩いて行ったそうです。

どうして why; for what reason

いい音がでない (it) does not sound good [いい (good; fine; nice) + 音 (sound) + が (identifies what performs the action; emphasizes the preceding word) + でない (plain negative form of でる (to come out))]

のか (indirect question marker) [emphasizes uncertainty or doubts and is used when you request a clearer or more precise answer from the other person]

調べてもらいました examined (it) for me [from 調べる (to examine; to look up; to investigate; to check up); ～てもらいました is the polite past form of ～てもらう (to get somebody to do something); how to form: Verb て-form + もらいました]

その当時は at that time; back then; in those days [その (that; the) + 当時 (at that time; in those days) + は (adds emphasis)]

自動車 car; automobile; motorcar

電車 train; electric train

自動車も電車も走っていません there were no cars or trains [自動車も電車も (neither cars nor trains; 「Xも～Yも」 means "neither X nor Y") + 走っていません (not running; polite negative form of 走っている (ている form of 走る (to run); which is used to describe a continuous action))]

から so; since; because

オルガンを担いで carry the organ [オルガン (organ) + を (indicates the direct object of action) + 担いで (て-form of 担ぐ (to shoulder; to carry on one's shoulder) which is used to connect to the next phrase)]

東京まで歩いて行った went on foot to Tokyo [東京 (Tokyo) + まで (to; up to) + 歩いて行った (went on foot; plain past form of 歩いて行く (go on foot; walk; 歩いて (て-form of 歩く (to walk) which is used to connect to the next verb 行く) + 行く (to go)))]

そうです it is said that ～; (I) heard that ～; it appears

そこで、「調律ができていません。」と言われました。山葉

は、それまで音学や音階、音楽理論など勉強したことがありま

せんでしたから、１か月東京に残って、音楽の勉強をしたそ

うです。

そこで　there [そこ (there) + で (indicates the location of action)]

「調律ができていません。」"(It's) not in tune." [「」 (quotation marks; " ") + 調律 (tuning (musical)) + が (is used with potential form of verb) + できていません (is not; unable; couldn't; polite negative form of できている (ている form of できる (to be able to do) which is used to describe the actual condition or appearance of the subject); how to form: Verb て-form + いません)]

「調律ができていません。」と言われました (he) was told, "(It's) not in tune." [「調律ができていません。」("(It's) not in tune.") + と (quotation marker) + 言われました (polite passive positive past form of 言う (to say; to utter))]

それまで　until then; up to that time [それ (that; it) + まで (until (a time); up to; till; to)]

音学や音階 science of sound, and musical scale [音学 (science of sound) + や (and; or; connecting particle; how to form: Noun + や + Noun) + 音階 (musical scale)]

音楽理論　music theory; logic of music

など　et cetera; etc.; and the like

勉強したことがありませんでした (he) had never studied (it) before [from 勉強する (to study); ～たことがありませんでした is the polite negative past form of ～たことがある (have done something before); how to form: Verb-plain past + ことがありませんでした]

から　so; because; since

1か月 a month; one month

東京に残って stay in Tokyo [東京 (Tokyo) + に (indicates the location of existence) + 残って (て-form of 残る (to stay; to remain) which is used to connect to the next phrase)]

音楽の勉強をした studied music [音楽 (music) + の (of; modifier) + 勉強 (study; lesson) + を (indicates the direct object of action) + した (plain past form of する (to do; to carry out))]

そうです　it is said that ~; (I) heard that ~; it appears

その後、１９００年には、日本で初めてのピアノを作りまし

た。この時、協力したのが河合小市という人で、ヤマハにつ

ぐピアノ製造会社「KAWAI」の創業者です。

その後 later; after that (time); then; thereafter

1900年には in 1900; in the year 1900 [年 (year) + には (in; puts more emphasis and restriction on the preceding word)]

日本で in Japan [日本 (Japan) + で (in)]

初めてのピアノを作りました built the first piano (in Japan) [初めて (first; first time) + の (of; modifier) + ピアノ (piano) + を (indicates the direct object of action) + 作りました (built; polite past form of 作る (to build; to make; to produce))]

この時 at this time; in this instance [この (this) + 時 (time; moment)]

協力したのが the (person) who cooperated [協力した (cooperated; plain past form of 協力する (work cooperatively; work together; cooperate); a relative clause that modifies the placeholder "の") + の (is a particle that acts like a noun; placeholder for nouns; how to form: Relative clause + の) ＋ が (emphasizes the preceding word)]

河合小市という人で the person named Kawai Koichi [河合小市 (Kawai Koichi) + という (named; called) + 人 (person) + で (て-form of です (be; is) which is used to connect to the next phrase)]

ヤマハにつぐ after Yamaha; next to Yamaha [ヤマハ (Yamaha) + に (to) + つぐ (to rank next to; to come after)]

ピアノ製造会社「KAWAI」の創業者 the founder of "KAWAI", the piano manufacturer (next to Yamaha) [ピアノ (piano) + 製造会社 (manufacturer; manufacturing company) + 「KAWAI」 ("KAWAI") + の (of; modifier) + 創業者 (founder (of a company))]

です be; is

山葉寅楠は、とてもまじめで几帳面な人だったそうです。

さて、ヤマハという会社は楽器作りで世界的に有名になりますが、楽器だけではありません。ヤマハは、エンジンを作っている会社でもあります。

とても very; exceedingly

まじめで几帳面な人 a serious and meticulous person [まじめ (serious; honest; sober; earnest) + で (て-form of です (be; is) which is used to connect to the next phrase, creating the meaning of "and") + 几帳面な (methodical; precise; meticulous) + 人 (person; man; people)]

だった was [plain past form of です (be; is)]

そうです it is said that ~; (I) heard that ~; it appears

さて by the way; well; now; then

ヤマハという会社は the company called Yamaha [ヤマハ (Yamaha; Yamaha Corporation) + という (called; named) + 会社 (company; corporation) + は (indicates the sentence topic)]

楽器作りで for making musical instruments [楽器 (musical instrument) + 作り (making; producing; manufacturing) + で (in; for; is used to express ranges)]

世界的に worldwide; global; international; world-class

有名になります become famous [有名 (famous) + に (expresses the result of change) + なります (ます/ polite form of なる (to become; to attain; to turn))]

が but; however

楽器だけではありません not only for musical instruments [楽器 (musical instrument) + だけではありません (not only; だけ (only; just) + ではありません (not; polite negative form of です (be; is)))]

エンジンを作っている会社 a company that makes engines [エンジン (engine) + を (indicates the direct object of action) + 作っている (make; is/are creating; ている-form of 作る (to make; to create; to produce) which is used to describe a continuous action) + 会社 (company; corporation)]

でもあります is also [も (too; also) is placed after で because the で part of the copula であります (be; is) can stick to the particle も]

ヤマハのバイク、ボートご存知ですよね。楽器作りの会社がな

ぜバイクやボートを作るようになったのでしょうか？

次回はそのお話をしたいと思います。

ヤマハのバイク Yamaha motorcycles [ヤマハ (Yamaha) + の (of; 's; modifier) + バイク (motorcycle; motorbike; bike)]

ボート boat; rowing boat

ご存知 knowing [honorific or respectful language]

ですよね right?; you know; isn't it so?

楽器作りの会社が a company that makes musical instruments [楽器 (musical instrument) + 作り (making; producing; manufacturing; building) + の (of; modifier) + 会社 (company; corporation) + が (identifies what performs the action; emphasizes the preceding word)]

なぜ why; how

バイクやボートを作る to make motorcycles and boats [バイク (motorcycle; motorbike; bike) + や (and; such things as ...) + ボート (boat; rowing boat) + を (indicates the direct object of action) + 作る (to make; to produce; to manufacture)]

ようになった came to be that; turned into ~; reached the point that [plain past form of ようになる (to come to be that); how to form: Verb (dictionary form) + ようになった]

のでしょうか (ask a question in a polite way) [how to form: Verb (casual) + のでしょうか]

次回は next time around [次回 (next time (occasion)) + は (adds emphasis)]

そのお話をしたいと思います (I) would like to talk about that [その (that; the) + お話 (talk; discussion) + を (indicates the direct object of action) + したい (want to do; from する (to do; to carry out); ~たい means "want to do something"; how to form: Verb (ます-stem form) + たい) + と思います (to think...; I think...; you think...)]

Yamaha

Please try to tackle the Japanese first and use this only as needed.

Do you know the company called Yamaha? Those who have studied music or have taken piano lessons know it well. It is the company with the largest sales volume of pianos in the world. Yamaha was started by a man named Yamaha Torakusu in the Meiji era (1868-1912). He started out repairing organs (musical instrument).

In 1887, Yamaha Torakusu was asked by an elementary school to repair an organ. It was an American-made organ. Since Yamaha had studied watch repair, he repaired that organ. He saw the structure of the organ and thought to try building one himself.

At that time, all organs were foreign-made and very expensive. The organ cost 45 yen at that time (about 900,000 yen today). But Yamaha said, "I'll make it myself for 3 yen!" And he was right. A year later, he built Japan's first domestically produced organ. However, when the teachers played it at school, they said, "It doesn't sound very good."

Yamaha took his self-made organ to the Music Investigation Office in Tokyo (now Tokyo University of the Arts) to find out why it did not sound good. At that time, there were no cars or trains, so he carried the organ on foot to Tokyo.

There, he was told, "It's not in tune." Yamaha had never studied the science of sound, musical scale, or music theory before, so he stayed in Tokyo for a month to study music.

Later, in 1900, he built the first piano in Japan. At this time, the person who cooperated in this project was Kawai Koichi, the founder of "KAWAI", the second largest piano manufacturer after YAMAHA.

Yamaha Torakusu was a very serious and meticulous person. By the way, Yamaha is world famous for making musical instruments, but not only for musical instruments. Yamaha is also a company that makes engines. You know Yamaha motorcycles and boats, don't you?

How did a company that made musical instruments come to make motorcycles and boats?

I would like to talk about that in the next issue.

ヤマハ

　ヤマハという会社を知っていますか？音楽を勉強した人、ピアノを習った
ことのある人は、良く知っていると思います。ピアノの販売量が世界一の会社で
す。ヤマハは、明治時代、山葉寅楠という人が始めました。きっかけは、オルガ
ンの修理でした。

　１８８７年、山葉寅楠は、ある小学校からオルガンの修理を頼まれました。
アメリカ製のオルガンでした。山葉は、時計の修理などを勉強していたので、こ
のオルガンを修理します。そのとき、オルガンの構造を見て、自分で作ってみよ
うと思いました。

　その頃、オルガンはすべて外国製でとても高価でした。このオルガンは当
時45円（今の約90万）でした。でも、山葉は、「自分なら3円で作ってみせ
る！」と言ったそうです。そして、言ったとおり、1年後に日本で初めての国産の
オルガンを作りました。ところが、学校で先生たちに弾いてもらうと、「あまり
いい音がしません。」と言われてしまいます。

　山葉は、東京の音楽取り調べ所（今の東京芸術大学）まで自作のオルガン
を運んで、どうしていい音がでないのか、調べてもらいました。その当時は、自
動車も電車も走っていませんから、オルガンを担いで東京まで歩いて行ったそう
です。

　そこで、「調律ができていません。」と言われました。山葉は、それまで

Continued

音学や音階、音楽理論など勉強したことがありませんでしたから、1か月東京に残って、音楽の勉強をしたそうです。

その後、1900年には、日本で初めてのピアノを作りました。この時、協力したのが河合小市という人で、ヤマハにつぐピアノ製造会社「KAWAI」の創業者です。

山葉寅楠は、とてもまじめで几帳面な人だったそうです。

さて、ヤマハという会社は楽器作りで世界的に有名になりますが、楽器だけではありません。ヤマハは、エンジンを作っている会社でもあります。ヤマハのバイク、ボート、ご存知ですよね。

楽器作りの会社がなぜバイクやボートを作るようになったのでしょうか？

次回はそのお話をしたいと思います。

Kanji in Focus

It is usually helpful to create a story based on the meanings of the kanji parts. Often, different kanji learning systems will use different "meanings" for the parts. We try to give the most common ones, but consistency is best. Choose one meaning per kanji part and stick with it. The following are a selection of the kanji found in this story. The <u>under-lined</u> reading is probably the most used.

楽	**READINGS** **MEANING** **EXAMPLE**	<u>ガク</u>・ラク・ゴウ・たのしい・たのしむ・このむ music; comfort; ease おんがく 音楽 music	冫 ice 白 white 木 tree; shrub; bush; wood This creative **ice** 冫 cream themed **white** 白 Christmas **tree** 木 brings *comfort* to a lonely child.
量	**READINGS** **MEANING** **EXAMPLE**	<u>リョウ</u>・はかる quantity; measure; weight; amount はんばいりょう 販売量 sales volume	日 sun; day 一 one 里 *ri* (old Japanese unit of distance about 2.44 miles) The *amount* he paid is enough for a **day** 日 trip of a less than **one** 一 *ri* 里 distance.
修	**READINGS** **MEANING** **EXAMPLE**	<u>シュウ</u>・シュ・おさめる・おさまる discipline; conduct one-self well; study; master しゅうり 修理 repair; mending; fixing; servicing	亻 person; man; human 丨 line; vertical stroke; rod 攵 strike; hit; folding chair 彡 three; hair ornament; short hair; fur That **man** 亻 wants to *master* the use of a **rod** 丨 to **hit** 攵 the **three** 彡 balls.
製	**READINGS** **MEANING** **EXAMPLE**	<u>セイ</u> made in...; manufacture せい アメリカ製 American-made	牛 cattle; cow; bull; ox 冂 upside-down box 刂 knife; standing sword 衣 clothes; garment; robe; gown They *manufacture* bottles for **cow's** 牛 milk, and store them inside an **upside-down box** 冂 that contains a **knife** 刂 and a white **robe** 衣.
価	**READINGS** **MEANING** **EXAMPLE**	<u>カ</u>・ケ・あたい value; price こうか 高価 highly priced; ex-pensive; valuable; costly	亻 person; man; human 西 west A **person** 亻 from the **west** 西 island had paid the *price* for it.

Kanji in Focus Continued

構	READINGS MEANING EXAMPLE	コウ・かまえる・かまう posture; build; pretend こうぞう 構造 structure; construction; makeup; framework	木 tree; shrub; bush; wood 冓 put together, inner palace Let's *build* a unique **tree 木** house in the **inner palace 冓**.
弾	READINGS MEANING EXAMPLE	ダン・タン・ひく・~ひき・はずむ・たま・はじく・はじける・ただす・はじきゆみ bullet; twang; flip; snap ひ 弾く to play (a stringed or keyboard instrument)	弓 bow (weapon); archery ⺍ small 田 field; rice field 十 ten; 10 The one who can find the lost *bullet* and **bow 弓** in the **small ⺍ rice field 田** will receive **ten 十** awards.
調	READINGS MEANING EXAMPLE	チョウ・しらべる・しらべ・ととのう・ととのえる tune; tone; meter; key (music); investigate ちょうりつ 調律 tuning (musical)	言 word; remark; statement 冂 upside-down box 土 earth; soil; dirt; clay; mud 口 mouth; opening; hole; gap *Investigate* his **statement 言** about an **upside-down box 冂** filled with **dirt 土** and without a **hole 口**.
帳	READINGS MEANING EXAMPLE	チョウ・とばり notebook; account book; album; curtain きちょうめん 几帳面 methodical; precise; meticulous	巾 width; breadth; towel; cloth 長 long; leader; superior; senior Cover the *book* with fine **cloth 巾** and give it to your **superior 長**.
約	READINGS MEANING EXAMPLE	ヤク・つづまる promise; approximately; shrink やく 約 approximately; about	糸 thread; yarn; string 勹 wrapping; wrap; embrace 丶 dot; tick The **yarn 糸** for **wrapping 勹** costs *approximately* as much as a **dot 丶**.

Do you have any questions? Anything confusing? Feel free to email me (Clay) at clay@thejapanshop.com with any questions, comments, or suggestions.

Do you have ideas to make *Makoto* better? We'd love to hear from you. Did something particularly help you? Love to hear that as well.

What to experience even more Makoto? Learn about our new Makoto+ membership. Download the latest issue or access web-based back issues. All this and more starting at only $3. Go to: **www.MakotoPlus.com** now!

Clay & Yumi